LET'S TALK

FEELING ANGRY

by Joy Berry • Illustrated by Maggie Smith

SCHOLASTIC INC.
New York Toronto London Auckland Sydney

ISBN 0-590-62386-9

Text copyright © 1995 by Joy Berry.
Illustrations copyright © 1995 by Scholastic Inc.
All rights reserved. Published by Scholastic Inc.

20 19 18 17 16 15 14 13   1 2 3 4 5 6/0

Printed in the U.S.A.   24
First Scholastic printing, November 1995

Hello, my name is Max.

I live with Maria.

Sometimes things don't happen
the way Maria wants them to happen.

Maria feels angry.

Sometimes people do things that hurt Maria.

Maria feels angry.

Sometimes people use Maria's things without asking.

Maria feels angry.

Sometimes people lose or break Maria's things.

Maria feels angry.

When you feel angry, you feel bad-tempered.

When you feel angry, you might want to do things you shouldn't do.

Try to avoid breaking things when you are angry.

Try to avoid doing things that could hurt you when you are angry.

Try to avoid doing things that could hurt other people when you are angry.

When you are angry, there are things you can do to make yourself feel better.

Try to calm down before doing anything.

Slowly counting to ten will give you time to calm down.

Talk to the person you are angry with.

Tell the person why you feel the way you do.

Ask the person to stop doing what's making you angry.

Sometimes the person who is making you angry won't listen to you.

Talk to a grown-up you know and trust.

Tell that person how you feel. Ask him or her to help you decide what you should do about your anger.

Sometimes you might need to do something with your energy when you are angry. It's okay for you to

Cry or yell,

Jump up and down, or

Hit something that can't be damaged — like a pillow, a punching bag, or your bed.

Avoid bothering anyone else while you are crying, yelling, jumping up and down, or hitting things.

When you are angry you might need to go outside.

Or

you might need to go into a room by yourself and close the door.

Remember that everyone gets angry.

Feeling angry is okay.

The important thing is to handle your anger in a positive way.